D0919427

Butterflies

Julie Murray

ABDO
Publishing Company

VISIT US AT
www.abdopublishing.com

Published by ABDO Publishing Company, 8000 West 78th Street, Edina, Minnesota 55439.

Printed in the United States of America, North Mankato, Minnesota.
042010
092010

Coordinating Series Editor: Rochelle Baltzer
Editor: Sarah Tieck
Contributing Editors: Heidi M.D. Elston, Megan M. Gunderson, BreAnn Rumsch, Marcia Zappa
Graphic Design: Maria Hosley
Cover Photograph: *iStockphoto*: ©iStockphoto.com/JodiJacobson.
Interior Photographs/Illustrations: *iStockphoto*: ©iStockphoto/CathyKeifer (p. 23), ©iStockphoto.com/cyfrogcione (p. 5), ©iStockphoto.com/kephotoman (p. 15), ©iStockphoto.com/Liliboas (p. 7), ©iStockphoto.com/PaulTessier (p. 13) ©iStockphoto.com/RichVintage (p. 29), ©iStockphoto.com/Silvrshootr (p. 15); *John Foxx Images* (p. 8); *Peter Arnold, Inc.*: ©Biosphoto/Héras Joël (pp. 24, 25), (droits geres); Gilson Francois (p. 30), D. Harms (p. 12), Matt Meadows (p. 15), C. Allan Morgan (p. 30), Bill OConnor (p. 17), Fritz Polking (p. 27), Ed Reschke (p. 15), Kevin Schafer (p. 8), Usher, D. (p. 21); *Photo Researchers, Inc.*: E.R. Degginger (p. 9), Eileen Tanson (p. 19); *Photodisc* (p. 27); *Shutterstock*: anotherlook (p. 27), Tom Grundy (p. 27), Ken Schulze (p. 9); Toenne (p. 11).

Library of Congress Cataloging-in-Publication Data

Murray, Julie, 1969-
Butterflies / Julie Murray.
p. cm. -- (Insects)
ISBN 978-1-61613-483-9
1. Butterflies--Juvenile literature. I. Title. II. Series: Murray, Julie, 1969- Insects.
QL544.2M87 2011
595.78'9--dc22

2010000787

Contents

Insect World

Insects are the largest group of living things. There are millions more insects than humans on Earth. Insects are found on the ground, in the air, and in the water.

Butterflies are one type of insect. They live in many different places, including jungles, woods, and fields. You may even find butterflies in a city or in your backyard!

Bug Bite!

Butterflies are closely related to moths.

There are many different types of butterflies. Some are very colorful.

A Butterfly's Body

Like all insects, a butterfly has three main body parts. These are the head, the **thorax**, and the **abdomen**.

A butterfly's head has two large eyes, two antennae, and a mouth. The mouth is a long tube, like a straw. It is called a proboscis (pruh-BAH-suhs).

Six legs and four wings connect to the thorax. The abdomen holds important **organs**.

Bug Bite!

Butterflies use their antennae to smell. This helps them find food.

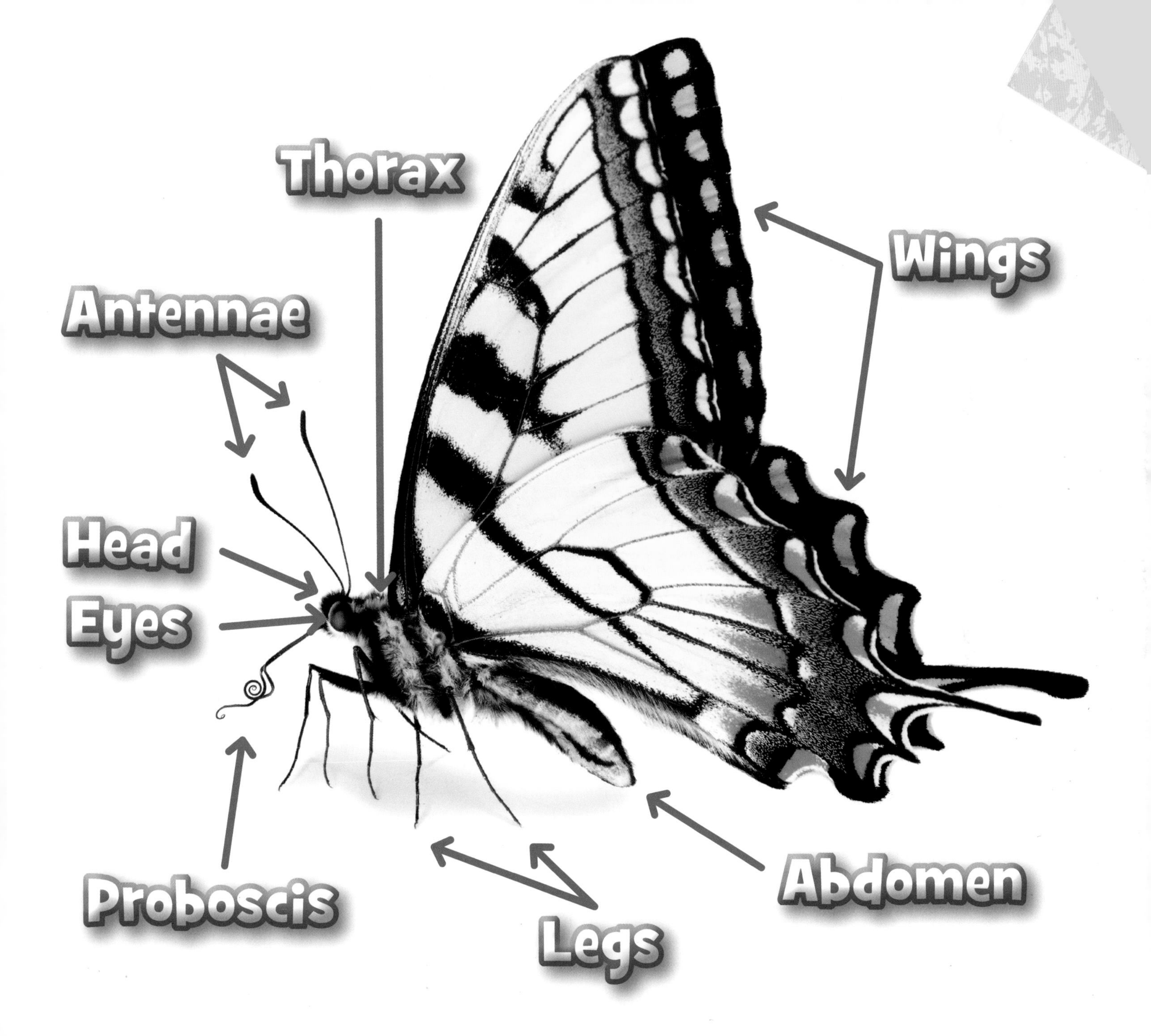
Thorax
Wings
Antennae
Head
Eyes
Proboscis
Legs
Abdomen

Beautiful Wings

Scales create the patterns on a butterfly's wings.

Up close, a butterfly's scales (*above*) look like shingles on a house roof (*right*).

A butterfly's wings make it look different from other insects. Many have colorful patterns.

Tiny scales cover a butterfly's wings. The scales do important work. For example, they take in the sun's heat to help warm the butterfly.

Fly Away Home

Butterflies live among flowers, bushes, and other plants. At night, they rest in safe or hidden areas.

During the day, butterflies drink flower nectar or other liquids. To drink, a butterfly uses its proboscis like a straw.

A butterfly stretches out its proboscis to drink nectar.

In Europe, peacock butterflies hibernate during winter months. They find safe spots in hollow trees, rock openings, and even houses.

Butterflies **protect** their bodies from rain, snow, and cold weather. Some butterflies sleep or rest during winter months. This is called hibernating.

In North America, monarch butterflies migrate every winter. They fly up to 1,900 miles (3,000 km) south to California and Mexico.

Other butterflies fly to warm places during winter. Some **migrate** thousands of miles!

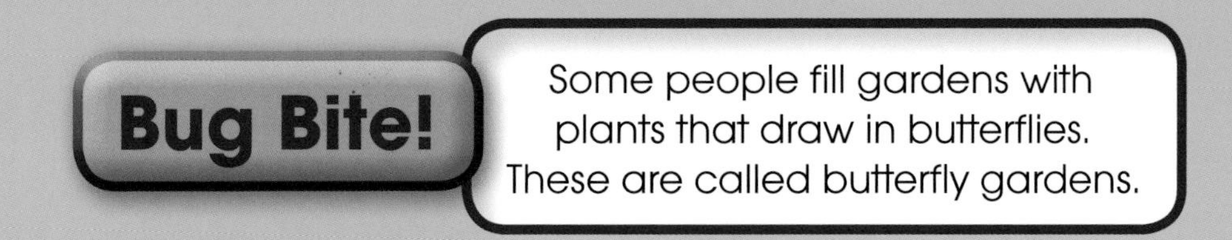

Life Begins

A butterfly goes through four different life stages. These stages are egg, larva, pupa, and adult. A butterfly larva is also called a caterpillar.

A butterfly begins life on land. Once it has become an adult, it can fly!

Life Cycle of a Monarch Butterfly

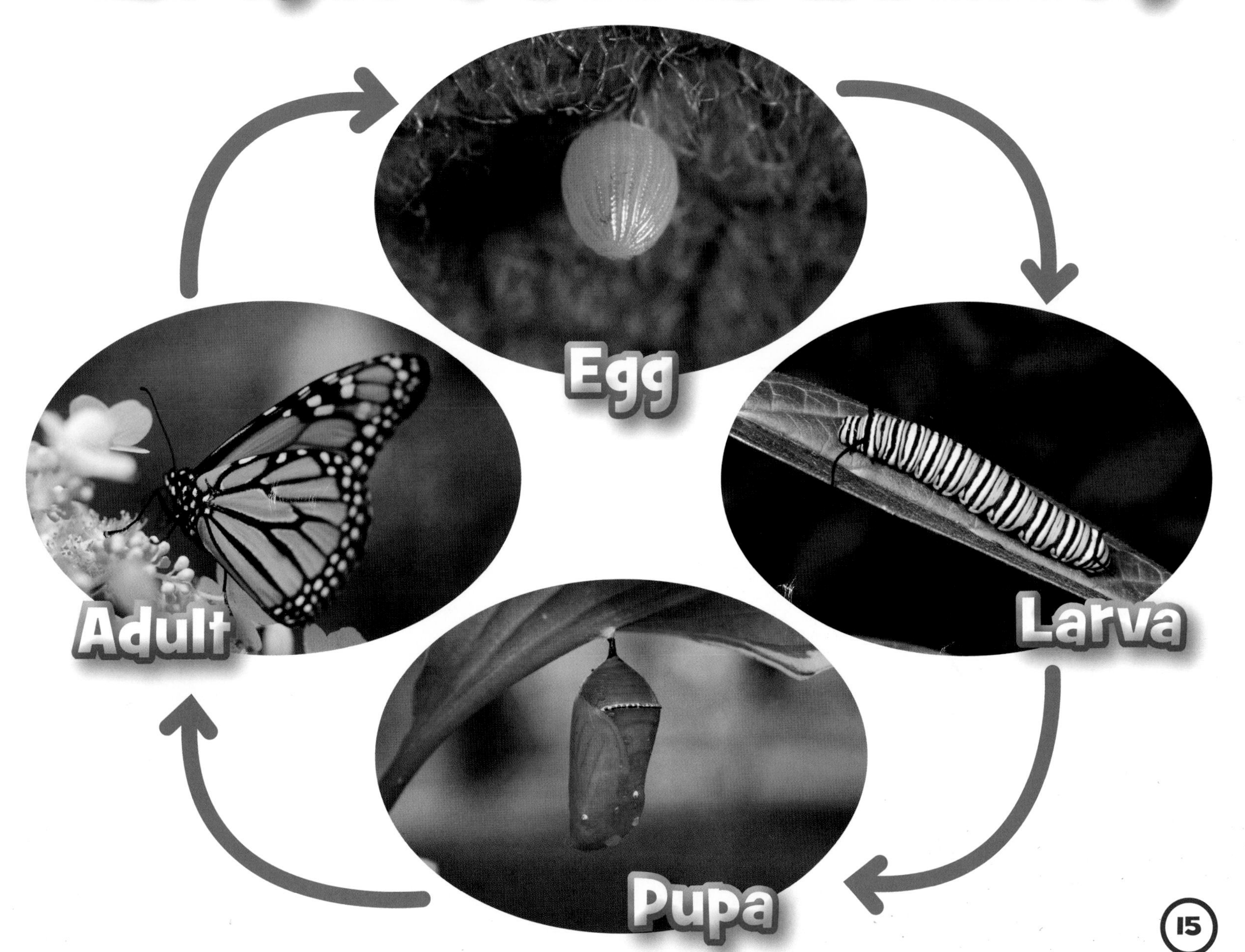

Egg to Caterpillar

A butterfly's life begins as an egg. Female and male butterflies **mate**. Then, mother butterflies lay their eggs.

A butterfly's egg is strong. It **protects** the caterpillar growing inside. An egg is also sticky. This helps it hold on to surfaces.

Bug Bite!

Some butterfly mothers drop their eggs while flying.

Most butterfly mothers choose a safe spot to lay their eggs. Many lay them on leaves.

A Caterpillar's Life

A caterpillar grows inside its egg until it is ready to **hatch**. Then, the caterpillar eats through its eggshell. It also eats nearby food. Most eat green plants.

When a caterpillar grows too big for its skin, it **sheds**. This happens several times while a caterpillar grows.

Some caterpillars start out as small as the head of a pin!

Caterpillars have many enemies. Monkeys, birds, and even people eat them!

Caterpillars **protect** themselves in different ways. Some can eat poisonous plants. This makes them taste bad to predators. Others hide or give off a bad smell.

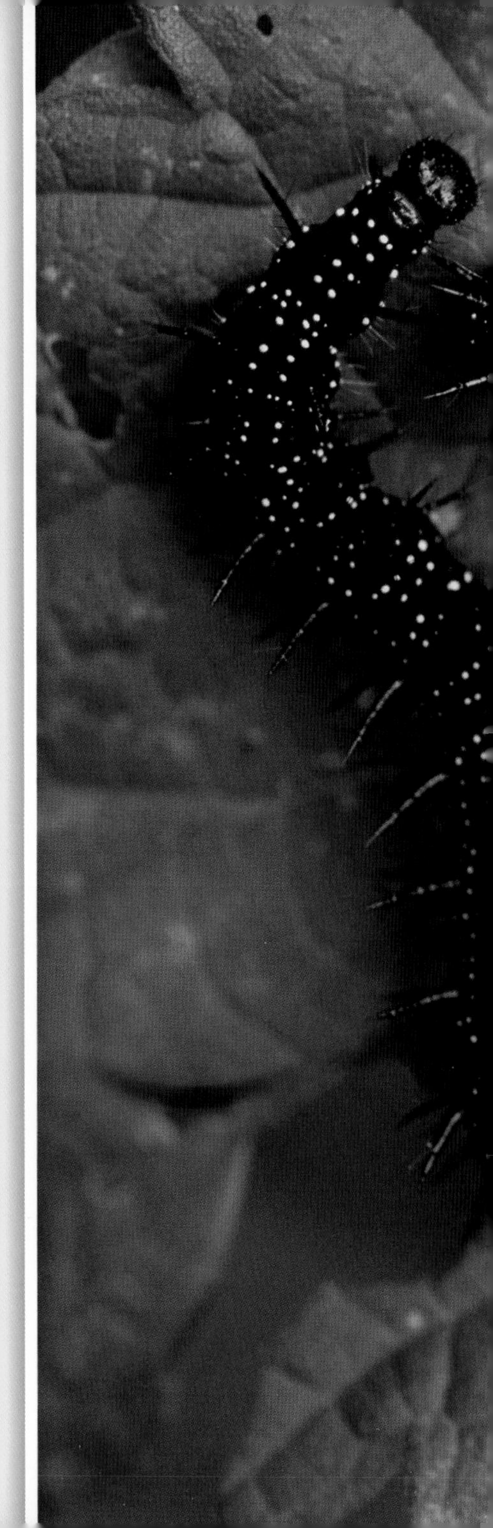

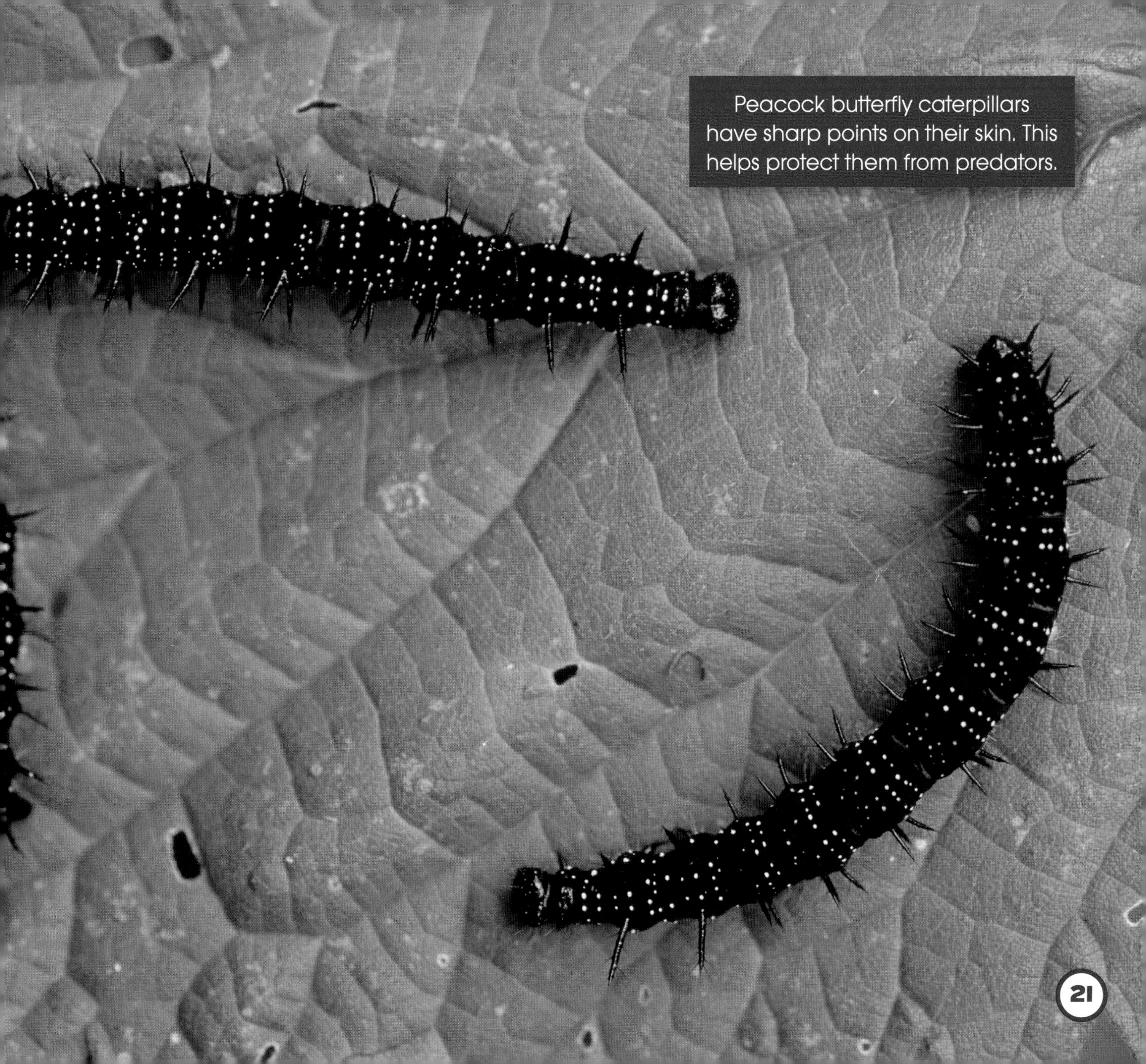

Peacock butterfly caterpillars have sharp points on their skin. This helps protect them from predators.

Inside the Chrysalis

A caterpillar eats for at least two weeks. Then it chooses a safe place, such as a tree branch.

There, a caterpillar **sheds** its skin one last time. Now it is a pupa. It has a hard shell known as a chrysalis (KRIH-suh-luhs). This covers its body.

A caterpillar's body changes to become a pupa.

The pupa stage may last from several days to more than a year. It is different for each **species**. Inside the chrysalis, wings and a new body form. Finally, the chrysalis breaks open and an adult butterfly comes out.

When a butterfly leaves its chrysalis, its wings are wrinkled. It must wait to fly.

A new butterfly's wings are soft and weak. The butterfly slowly fans its wings to harden them. Finally, it is ready to fly off into the world.

Danger Zone

Adult butterflies face many predators. These include birds, spiders, lizards, and rats.

Special body features **protect** butterflies. Some butterflies have round spots on their wings that look like eyes. This tricks predators. Others are brightly colored. Bright colors tell predators something is likely poisonous. So, they usually stay away.

The large spot on an owl butterfly's wings looks like an owl's eye.

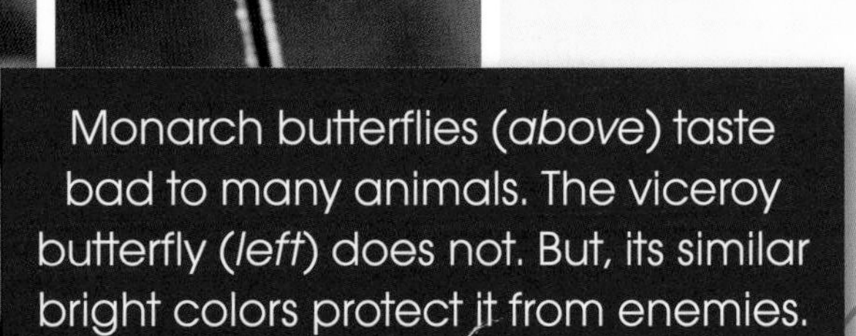

Monarch butterflies (*above*) taste bad to many animals. The viceroy butterfly (*left*) does not. But, its similar bright colors protect it from enemies.

A dead leaf butterfly hides on plants.

Special Insects

Butterflies do important work in the natural world. When they land on flowers, pollen sticks to their bodies. The pollen rubs off on the next flowers they land on. This movement of pollen is called pollination. It helps plants grow.

Some butterflies are in danger of dying out. Scientists work to save them. This helps **protect** life on Earth.

Bug Bite!

Sometimes, buildings or farms replace natural areas. This can hurt butterfly homes. And, it can put butterfly populations in danger.

To learn about butterflies, it is important to look closely but not touch.

Bug-O-Rama

What is the largest butterfly?

The Queen Alexandra's birdwing butterfly is the largest. It is about 11 inches (28 cm) from wingtip to wingtip. That's almost as long as a standard ruler!

What's a cool thing butterflies do?

Butterflies can taste with their feet! When some butterfly mothers are ready to lay eggs, they stand on leaves. This helps them taste test the leaves their caterpillars will **hatch** on.

Yuck! They do what?!

Many swallowtail butterfly caterpillars lie very still and pretend to be bird poop. This tricks predators.

Important Words

abdomen (AB-duh-muhn) the back part of an insect's body.

hatch to be born from an egg.

mate to join as a couple in order to reproduce, or have babies.

migrate to move from one place to another to find food or have babies.

organ a body part that does a special job. The heart and the lungs are organs.

protect (pruh-TEHKT) to guard against harm or danger.

shed to cast aside or lose as part of a natural process of life.

species (SPEE-sheez) living things that are very much alike.

thorax the middle part of an insect's body.

Web Sites

To learn more about butterflies, visit ABDO Publishing Company online. Web sites about butterflies are featured on our Book Links page. These links are routinely monitored and updated to provide the most current information available.

www.abdopublishing.com

Index